Practical
Hot & Spicy

p^3

This is a P³ Book
This edition published in 2003

P³
Queen Street House
4 Queen Street
Bath BA1 1HE, UK

ISBN: 1-40540-549-X

Printed in China

NOTE

This book uses metric and imperial measurements. Follow the same units
of measurement throughout; do not mix metric and imperial.
All spoon measurements are level: teaspoons are assumed to be 5 ml, and
tablespoons are assumed to be 15 ml. Unless otherwise stated,
milk is assumed to be full fat, eggs and individual vegetables such as potatoes
are medium, and pepper is freshly ground black pepper.

The nutritional information provided for each recipe is per serving or per person.
Optional ingredients, variations or serving suggestions have
not been included in the calculations. The times given for each recipe are an approximate
guide only because the preparation times may differ according to the techniques used by
different people and the cooking times may vary as a result of the type of oven used.

Recipes using raw or very lightly cooked eggs should be
avoided by children, the elderly, pregnant women, convalescents,
and anyone suffering from an illness.

Contents

Introduction

Changing tastes and a more daring approach to what we eat have led in recent years to a growing interest in food from many different cultures. Among the most popular cuisines are those from China, India, Thailand, Mexico – anywhere, in fact, that serves hot and spicy dishes, bursting with new and exciting flavours that sometimes make your eyes water as well as your mouth. Soups, fish, meat, chicken and vegetables are transformed with the addition of chillies, ginger and garlic, and with a range of dried spices. The recipes in this book are quick and easy to make, but still impressive: you can create something really inspirational for a special occasion, and you can even round it off with a hot and spicy dessert.

Storecupboard items

In the countries from which these recipes are taken, most of the ingredients are bought absolutely fresh from the daily markets. In Thailand the diet is mostly based on fish – caught, landed and sold within a very short time. Vegetables are also carefully chosen and purchased each day as needed.

However, there are some items that can be kept on hand. Rice is the most important staple food, either forming the basis of the main course or, more often, served as a side dish, perhaps with herbs, spices or vegetables added. Long-grain white rice and Indian basmati rice with its distinctive aroma and flavour are staples and readily available in supermarkets. They will keep for quite a while in an airtight container. Noodles are another staple, used frequently in Chinese and Thai cooking where they are tossed in a wok with meat or fish and vegetables, and seasoned generously. They come in many forms and among the most popular are rice noodles – almost transparent and shaped as flat ribbons or thin vermicelli – and the egg noodles favoured by the Chinese, which are a rich yellow in colour and crinkled in shape. Both types are not so much cooked as softened by soaking in boiling water for just a few minutes.

A range of oils is also useful, and some of these will already be kept in the storecupboard for general use.

Sunflower oil and vegetable oil are the most widely used, because they are light and mild, complementing the food rather than flavouring it. Olive oil is

commonly used in some cuisines, notably Mexican, and it is best to choose a really good extra-virgin olive oil. It is also worth investing in a bottle of sesame oil made from roasted sesame seeds and full of flavour. This is not used for cooking food because it burns easily. Instead, it is drizzled over the finished dish. And for the very brave, a bottle of chilli oil is hot stuff indeed.

Beans are often used as the basis of spicy dishes because they readily absorb the delicious flavours of the food. The classic is the ever-popular Mexican chilli-bean stew, warming and filling. When using beans you have two options: you can buy packets of dried beans, which are very cheap and keep well but have to be soaked overnight before cooking; or you can buy cans of ready-cooked beans, which are a little more expensive but very useful if you want to rustle up a quick dish for lunch or for an evening dish midweek.

Also readily available, and ideal for anyone with limited spare time, are the jars of sauces and pastes stocked by supermarkets everywhere. Using bottled sauces is not quite the same as making them from scratch, but they still taste good. Green and red Thai curry pastes can be used for a fast green fish curry or a red lamb curry. Indian curry pastes range from mild to extremely hot. Many of the recipes in this book need dried spices, such as cumin, coriander, cardamom and turmeric. Their flavour

deteriorates rapidly, so, unless you are planning to do a lot of this type of cooking, buy them in small quantities and store them in a cool, dark place. Also add some authentic seasoning sauces to your storecupboard – soy sauce, which is made from fermented soya beans, and Thai fish sauce, which is made from salted fermented fish.

Chillies, ginger and garlic

All these items add a real zing to your hot and spicy cooking, but it is fair to say that when it comes to heat, chillies are the star. There are many varieties of chilli, and different cultures favour different ones, so it is worth looking out for the right one for a particular dish. Many recipes call for fresh chillies, but dried, crushed chillies may be substituted. Some chillies are quite mild, while others are fiery hot – large chillies are usually milder than small ones, and red chillies tend to be a little sweeter and milder than green ones. If you are in any doubt about eating a dish seasoned with chillies, bear in mind that most of the heat is in the seeds. If you remove the seeds before cooking, the dish will not be so fiery.

Thai dishes often include bird-eye chillies. These are small and either red or green, and they are very, very hot. In Mexico, where chillies of one variety or another are included in virtually every recipe, the small, green variety called *jalapeño* is especially popular, and dried chillies – *ancho* and *chipotle* – are also used.

Chillies are extremely irritating to the skin, so if you are particularly sensitive, wear rubber gloves when preparing them, and if you are removing the seeds, do so with the point of a sharp knife. Always wash your hands really thoroughly afterwards, and make sure you keep your hands away from your eyes.

Fresh ginger is a wonderful spice, adding flavour as well as fire. Substituting the dried, powdered ginger used in baking is out of the question. The fresh or 'green' root is sold in supermarkets everywhere, however, and your only problem may be in identifying it. It is quite small and very knobbly, similar to a Jerusalem artichoke in shape and colour, and it should feel firm to the touch.

When the root is peeled, the yellow flesh is revealed and the delicious aroma wafts out. Ginger is usually grated and thrown into the wok at the start of cooking a stir-fry, infusing the oil with its marvellous flavour.

Garlic, crushed or chopped, is used throughout the world, and not just for spicy cooking, so fresh garlic is usually readily available. It is a bulb formed of edible cloves packed tightly around an inedible core. Garlic's reputation for tainting the breath is unfortunately entirely justified, but you may decide that the special flavour and subtle kick it imparts is worth it – chewing parsley or caraway seeds is said to reduce the odour.

Cooking utensils

There is no essential piece of equipment needed for hot and spicy cuisine – your usual saucepans and a good heavy frying pan will be all you need – but if you intend to do a lot of spicy cooking, a wok is a very useful item of equipment to have in the kitchen. The wok is a Chinese cooking pan. It is shallow and convex in shape, allowing the heat to spread evenly, especially if it sits on a 'collar' over the heat source. It is ideal for stir-frying because the curved sides make it easy to toss food as it cooks. For this you need a spatula with a long wooden

handle to insulate your hand from the heat. Although they are pricey, it is worth investing in a cast-iron wok, because these are most effective at retaining heat – and fast cooking is the key to successful stir-frying.

The wok is at its best when well seasoned. To do this, wipe it inside and out with oil, then bring it up to a high temperature on a stove. Repeat this a few times to coat it well. The seasoned wok will then only need to be wiped after use, then cleaned with soap and water and dried immediately to prevent rusting.

KEY		
	Simplicity level 1–3 (1 easiest, 3 slightly harder)	
	Preparation time	
	Cooking time	

Mexican Chilli Soup

This soup evolved from the food stalls that line the streets of Tlalpan, a suburb of Mexico City. It contains avocado, chicken and chipotle chillies.

NUTRITIONAL INFORMATION

Calories 218	Sugars 1g	
Protein 28g	Fat 11g	
Carbohydrate 2g	Saturates 2g	

🥑 15 mins   🕐 0 mins

SERVES 4

I N G R E D I E N T S

1.5 litres/2¾ pints chicken stock

2–3 garlic cloves, finely chopped

1–2 chipotle chillies, cut into very thin strips (see Cook's Tip)

1 avocado

lime or lemon juice, for tossing

3–5 spring onions, thinly sliced

350–400 g/12–14 oz cooked chicken breast meat, torn, or cut into shreds or thin strips

2 tbsp chopped fresh coriander

TO SERVE

1 lime, cut into wedges

handful of tortilla chips (optional)

1 Pour the stock in a large pan, with the garlic and the chipotle chillies, and bring to the boil.

2 Meanwhile, cut the avocado in half around the stone. Twist apart, then remove the stone with a knife. Carefully peel away the skin, dice the flesh and toss it gently in lime or lemon juice to prevent discoloration.

3 Arrange the spring onions, chicken, avocado and coriander in the bottom of 4 soup bowls or in a large serving bowl.

4 Ladle the hot stock over the ingredients in the bowls and serve with wedges of lime, and a handful of tortilla chips, if using.

COOK'S TIP

Chipotle chillies are smoked and dried jalapeño chillies and are available canned or dried.

Hot & Sour Soup

Hot-and-sour mixtures are popular throughout the East, especially in Thailand. This soup typically has either prawns or chicken added.

NUTRITIONAL INFORMATION

Calories 71   Sugars 0.1g
Protein . . . . .8g   Fat 4g
Carbohydrate . . . .1g   Saturates 0.1g

30 mins   25 mins

SERVES 4

INGREDIENTS

350 g/12 oz whole raw or cooked prawns in their shells

1 tbsp vegetable oil

1 lemon grass stalk, roughly chopped

2 kaffir lime leaves, shredded

1 green chilli, deseeded and chopped

1.2 litres/2 pints chicken or fish stock

1 lime

1 tbsp Thai fish sauce

1 red bird-eye chilli, deseeded and thinly sliced

1 spring onion, thinly sliced

salt and pepper

1 tbsp finely chopped fresh coriander, to garnish

1 Peel the prawns and reserve the shells. Devein the prawns, cover and chill.

2 Heat the oil in a large pan and stir-fry the prawn shells for 3–4 minutes until they turn pink. Add the lemon grass, lime leaves, green chilli and stock. Grate the zest from the lime and add to the pan.

3 Bring to the boil, then lower the heat, cover and simmer the stock gently for about 20 minutes.

4 Strain the liquid, then pour it back into the pan. Squeeze the juice from the lime and add to the pan with the fish sauce, and salt and pepper to taste.

5 Bring the soup to the boil. Lower the heat, add the prawns and simmer for just 2–3 minutes.

6 Add the red chilli and spring onion. Sprinkle with coriander and serve.

COOK'S TIP

To devein the prawns, first remove the shells. Cut a slit along the back of each prawn and remove the fine black vein that runs along the length of the back. Wipe each prawn with clean kitchen paper.

Authentic Guacamole

Guacamole is at its best when it is freshly made. Serve it as a sauce with anything Mexican, or as a dip for raw vegetable sticks or tortilla chips.

NUTRITIONAL INFORMATION

Calories	212	Sugars	.........1g
Protein	.........2g	Fat	..........21g
Carbohydrate	....3g	Saturates	.......4g

15 mins   0 mins

SERVES 4

I N G R E D I E N T S

1 ripe tomato

2 limes

2–3 ripe, small to medium avocados, or 1–2 large ones

¼–½ onion, finely chopped

pinch of ground cumin

pinch of mild chilli powder

½–1 green chilli, such as jalapeño or serrano, deseeded and finely chopped

1 tbsp finely chopped fresh coriander, plus extra to garnish

salt (optional)

tortilla chips, to serve (optional)

1 First skin the tomato: place it in a bowl, cover with boiling water and leave to stand for 30 seconds. Drain and plunge the tomato into cold water. The skin will then slide off easily. Cut in half, deseed, and chop the tomato flesh.

2 Squeeze the juice from the limes into a small bowl. Cut the avocados in half around the stones. Twist apart, then remove the stones with a knife. Carefully peel off the skin, dice the flesh and toss in the bowl of lime juice to prevent them from discolouring. Mash the avocados coarsely.

3 Add the onion, tomato, cumin, chilli powder, chopped chillies and chopped coriander to the mashed avocados. If the guacamole is to be used as a dip for tortilla chips, do not add salt. If it is to be used as a sauce, add salt to taste.

4 To serve the guacamole as a dip, transfer it to a serving dish, garnish with finely chopped coriander and serve with tortilla chips for dipping.

COOK'S TIP

Avocados grow in abundance in Mexico, and guacamole is used to add richness and flavour to all manner of dishes. Try spooning it into soups, especially chicken or seafood, or spreading it into sandwiches or on thick, crusty rolls.

Grilled Aubergine

Aubergines grow easily throughout the Far East and they are a popular vegetable in Thailand. This dish works well as a first course.

NUTRITIONAL INFORMATION

Calories 106   Sugars 6g
Protein . . . . .3g   Fat 8g
Carbohydrate . . . .7g   Saturates 1g

20 mins, plus
50 mins salting   10 mins
and marinating

SERVES 4

INGREDIENTS

8 baby aubergines

salt, for salting aubergines

2 tsp chilli oil

1 tbsp soy sauce

1 tbsp Thai fish sauce

1 garlic clove, thinly sliced

1 red bird-eye chilli, deseeded and sliced

1 tbsp sunflower oil

1 tsp sesame oil

1 tbsp lime juice

1 tsp soft, light brown sugar

1 tbsp chopped fresh mint

1 tbsp sesame seeds, toasted

fresh mint leaves, to garnish

1 Cut the aubergines lengthways into thin slices to within 2.5 cm/1 inch of the stem end. Place the slices in a colander, sprinkle salt between them and leave to drain for about 30 minutes. Rinse under cold running water, then pat completely dry with kitchen paper.

2 Mix the chilli oil, soy sauce and fish sauce and brush over the aubergines. Cook under a hot grill, or barbecue over hot coals, for 6–8 minutes, turning occasionally and brushing with chilli oil glaze until golden and softened. Arrange the aubergines on a large serving platter.

3 Cook the sliced garlic and chilli in the sunflower oil for 1–2 minutes until they just begin to brown. Remove from the heat and add the sesame oil, lime juice, sugar and any remaining chilli oil glaze.

4 Add the chopped mint and spoon the warm dressing over the aubergines.

5 Leave to marinate for 20 minutes, then sprinkle with toasted sesame seeds. Serve garnished with mint leaves.

Spicy Lentils & Spinach

This is a filling dish, which should be served with just a light main course or as a one-dish lunch or supper. Split green peas are a type of lentil.

NUTRITIONAL INFORMATION

Calories 355	Sugars 7g
Protein 20g	Fat 16g
Carbohydrate . . .35g	Saturates 2g

10 mins, plus 2 hrs soaking   35 mins

SERVES 4

I N G R E D I E N T S

225 g/8 oz split green peas

900 g/2 lb spinach

4 tbsp vegetable oil

1 onion, halved and sliced

1 tsp grated fresh root ginger

1 tsp ground cumin

½ tsp chilli powder

½ tsp ground coriander

2 garlic cloves, crushed

300 ml/10 fl oz vegetable stock

salt and pepper

TO GARNISH

sprigs of fresh coriander

lime wedges

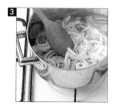

1 Rinse the split peas under cold running water. Transfer to a bowl, cover with cold water and soak for 2 hours. Drain well.

2 Meanwhile, cook the spinach in a large saucepan for 5 minutes until wilted. Drain well and chop roughly.

3 Heat the oil in a large saucepan and sauté the onion, spices and garlic. Sauté for 2–3 minutes, stirring well.

4 Add the split peas and spinach and stir in the stock. Cover and simmer for 10–15 minutes or until the split peas are cooked and the liquid has been absorbed. Season with salt and pepper to taste, garnish with sprigs of coriander and wedges of lime and serve.

VARIATION

If you do not have time to soak the split peas, canned puy lentils (drained) are a good substitute.

Mexican Potato Salad

This dish is full of enticing Mexican flavours. Potato slices are topped with tomatoes, chillies and peppers and served with a guacamole dressing.

NUTRITIONAL INFORMATION

Calories	260	Sugars	.........6g
Protein	.........6g	Fat	...........9g
Carbohydrate	...41g	Saturates	......2g

10 mins,
plus 30 mins
cooling

15 mins

SERVES 4

INGREDIENTS

4 large waxy potatoes, sliced

1 ripe avocado

1 tsp olive oil

1 tsp lemon juice

1 garlic clove, crushed

1 onion, chopped

2 large tomatoes, sliced

1 green chilli, chopped

1 yellow pepper, deseeded and cut
  into strips

2 tbsp chopped fresh coriander

salt and pepper

lemon wedges, to garnish

1 Cook the potatoes in a pan of boiling water for 15 minutes. Drain and cool.

2 Meanwhile, cut the avocado in half and remove the stone. Using a spoon, scoop the avocado flesh from the 2 halves and place in a mixing bowl.

3 Mash the avocado flesh with a fork. Stir in the olive oil, lemon juice, garlic and onion. Cover the bowl and set aside.

4 Mix the tomatoes, chilli, yellow pepper and potato slices, then divide them between serving plates.

5 Spoon the avocado mixture on top of the salad base and sprinkle over the coriander. Season to taste and serve garnished with lemon wedges.

COOK'S TIP

Choose a ripe avocado that yields to gentle pressure from your thumb. Mixing the avocado flesh with lemon juice prevents it from turning brown once exposed to the air.

Stir-fried Ginger Mushrooms

This quick vegetarian stir-fry is somewhat like a rich curry. It is full of warm spices and garlic, and the flavours are balanced with creamy coconut milk.

NUTRITIONAL INFORMATION

Calories 174   Sugars 7g
Protein ....8g   Fat 9g
Carbohydrate ...15g   Saturates 1g

   10 mins   10 mins

SERVES 4

INGREDIENTS

2 tbsp vegetable oil

3 garlic cloves, crushed

1 tbsp Thai red curry paste

½ tsp turmeric

425 g/15 oz canned Chinese straw
  mushrooms, drained and halved

2-cm/¾-inch piece fresh root ginger,
  finely shredded

100 ml/3½ oz coconut milk

40 g/1½ oz dried Chinese black mushrooms,
  soaked, drained and sliced

1 tbsp lemon juice

1 tbsp light soy sauce

2 tsp sugar

½ tsp salt

8 cherry tomatoes, halved

200 g/7 oz firm tofu, diced

fresh coriander leaves, to garnish

boiled fragrant rice, to serve

COOK'S TIP

You can vary the mushrooms
depending on your own taste. Try
a mixture of oyster and shiitake
for a change – or use cultivated
button mushrooms.

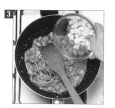

1 Heat the oil in a frying pan and cook the garlic for about 1 minute, stirring constantly. Stir in the curry paste and turmeric, and cook for another 30 seconds.

2 Add the straw mushrooms and ginger and stir-fry for 2 minutes. Stir in the coconut milk and bring to the boil. Add the Chinese black mushrooms, lemon juice, soy sauce, sugar and salt, stir well and heat thoroughly.

3 Add the tomatoes and tofu and toss gently to heat through.

4 Scatter the coriander over the mixture and serve hot with freshly boiled rice.

Spiced Cashew Nut Curry

This unusual vegetarian dish may be served on its own with rice, but can also be presented as a side dish with other vegetables or with meat.

NUTRITIONAL INFORMATION

Calories . . . . . . .455 Sugars 6g
Protein . . . . .13g Fat 39g
Carbohydrate . . .16g Saturates 11g

15 mins, plus
8 hrs soaking

20 mins

SERVES 4

INGREDIENTS

250 g/9 oz unsalted cashew nuts

1 tsp coriander seeds

1 tsp cumin seeds

2 cardamom pods, crushed

1 tbsp sunflower oil

1 onion, finely sliced

1 garlic clove, crushed

1 small green chilli, deseeded and chopped

1 cinnamon stick

½ tsp ground turmeric

4 tbsp coconut cream

300 ml/10 fl oz hot vegetable stock

3 kaffir lime leaves, finely shredded

salt and pepper

boiled jasmine rice, to serve

1 Soak the cashew nuts in cold water overnight. Drain thoroughly. Crush the coriander seeds, cumin seeds and cardamom pods in a spice grinder or with a pestle and mortar.

2 Heat the oil in a large frying pan and stir-fry the onion and garlic for about 2–3 minutes until they are soft but not brown. Add the chopped chilli, crushed spices, cinnamon stick and ground turmeric and stir-fry for another minute.

3 Add the coconut cream and the hot stock to the pan. Bring to the boil, then add the cashew nuts and lime leaves, and salt and pepper to taste.

4 Cover the pan, lower the heat and simmer for about 20 minutes. Remove and discard the cinnamon stick. Serve hot with freshly cooked jasmine rice.

COOK'S TIP

You can always use ready-ground spices for speed, but all spices will give a better flavour if you crush them just before use in a spice grinder or with a pestle and mortar.

Potato-filled Naan Breads

This is a filling sandwich made with Indian bread. Spicy potatoes fill the naans, which are served with a cool cucumber raita and lime pickle.

NUTRITIONAL INFORMATION

Calories 244   Sugars 7g
Protein ....8g   Fat 8g
Carbohydrate ...37g   Saturates 1g

10 mins   25 mins

SERVES 4

INGREDIENTS

225 g/8 oz waxy potatoes, scrubbed and diced

1 tbsp vegetable oil

1 onion, chopped

2 garlic cloves, crushed

1 tsp ground cumin

1 tsp ground coriander

½ tsp chilli powder

1 tbsp tomato purée

3 tbsp vegetable stock

75 g/2¾ oz baby spinach, shredded

4 small or 2 large naans

lime pickle, to serve

RAITA

150 ml/5 fl oz low-fat natural yogurt

4 tbsp diced cucumber

1 tbsp chopped mint

1 Cook the diced potatoes in a saucepan of boiling water for 10 minutes. Drain thoroughly.

2 Heat the vegetable oil in a separate saucepan and cook the onion and garlic for 3 minutes, stirring. Add the spices and cook for another 2 minutes.

3 Add the partially cooked potatoes, with the tomato purée, vegetable stock and spinach and stir to mix. Cook for 5 minutes until the potatoes are tender.

4 Warm the naans in a preheated oven, 150°C/300°F/Gas Mark 2, for about 2 minutes.

5 To make the raita, mix the yogurt, cucumber and mint together in a small bowl.

6 Remove the naans from the oven. Using a sharp knife, cut a pocket in the side of each. Spoon some of the spicy potato mixture into each pocket.

7 Serve the filled naans at once, accompanied by the raita and lime pickle.

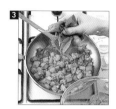

COOK'S TIP

To give the raita a much stronger flavour, make it in advance and leave to chill in the refrigerator until you are ready to serve the meal.

Migas

A delicious brunch or late-night supper dish, this is made by scrambling eggs with chillies, tomatoes and crisp tortilla chips.

  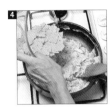

NUTRITIONAL INFORMATION

Calories 441   Sugars 5g
Protein . . . . .22g   Fat 20g
Carbohydrate . . .46g   Saturates 8g

 10 mins   10 mins

SERVES 4

I N G R E D I E N T S

2 tbsp butter

6 garlic cloves, finely chopped

1 fresh green chilli, such as jalapeño or serrano, deseeded and diced

1½ tsp ground cumin

6 ripe tomatoes, roughly chopped

8 eggs, lightly beaten

8–10 corn tortillas, cut into strips and fried until crisp, or an equal amount of not-too-salty tortilla chips

4 tbsp chopped fresh coriander

3–4 spring onions, thinly sliced

mild chilli powder, to garnish

1 Melt half the butter in a pan. Add the garlic and chilli and cook until softened but not browned. Add the cumin and cook for 30 seconds, stirring, then add the tomatoes and cook over a medium heat for an additional 3–4 minutes or until the tomato juices have evaporated. Remove from the pan and set aside.

2 Melt the remaining butter in a frying pan over a low heat and pour in the beaten eggs. Cook gently, stirring, until the egg begins to set.

3 Add the chilli and tomato mixture, stirring gently to mix into the eggs.

4 Carefully add the tortilla strips or chips and continue cooking, stirring once or twice, until the eggs have reached the consistency you desire. The tortillas should be pliable and chewy.

5 Transfer the mixture to a serving plate and surround it with the chopped coriander and sliced spring onions. Garnish with a sprinkling of mild chilli powder and serve immediately.

COOK'S TIP

Serve the migas with soured cream or crème fraîche on top, to melt seductively into the spicy eggs.

Mixed Vegetable Balti

Any combination of vegetables or beans can be used in this recipe.
It would make a good dish to serve to vegetarians.

NUTRITIONAL INFORMATION

Calories 207   Sugars 6g
Protein . . . . .8g   Fat 9g
Carbohydrate . . .24g   Saturates 1g

 10 mins   1 hr 10 mins

SERVES 4

I N G R E D I E N T S

225 g/8 oz split yellow peas, washed

3 tbsp oil

1 tsp onion seeds

2 onions, sliced

125 g/4½ oz courgettes, sliced

125 g/4½ oz potatoes, cut into
  1-cm/½-inch cubes

125 g/4½ oz carrots, sliced

1 small aubergine, sliced

225 g/8 oz tomatoes, chopped

300 ml/10 fl oz water

3 garlic cloves, chopped

1 tsp ground cumin

1 tsp ground coriander

1 tsp salt

2 fresh green chillies, sliced

½ tsp garam masala

2 tbsp chopped fresh coriander

1 Put the split peas into a pan and cover with salted water. Bring to the boil and simmer for 30 minutes. Drain the peas and keep warm.

2 Heat the oil in a balti pan or wok, and when it reaches a high temperature add the onion seeds. Keeping the heat high, cook them until they start popping.

3 Add the sliced onions and stir-fry until softened and golden brown.

4 Add the prepared courgettes, potatoes, carrots and aubergine to the pan and stir-fry for 2 minutes.

5 Stir in the chopped tomatoes, water, chopped garlic, ground cumin, ground coriander, salt, sliced chillies, garam masala and the reserved split peas.

6 Bring to the boil, then simmer for 15 minutes, stirring from time to time, until all the vegetables are tender.

7 Stir the coriander into the vegetables and serve.

Thai-spiced Salmon

Marinated in delicate Thai spices and quickly pan-fried to perfection, these salmon fillets are a perfect dish for a special dinner.

NUTRITIONAL INFORMATION

Calories	329	Sugars	.......0.1g
Protein	........30g	Fat	..........23g
Carbohydrate	...0.1g	Saturates	.......4g

15 mins, plus 30 mins chilling 5 mins

SERVES 4

INGREDIENTS

2.5-cm/1-inch piece grated fresh root ginger

1 tsp coriander seeds, crushed

¼ tsp chilli powder

1 tbsp lime juice

1 tsp sesame oil

4 medium salmon fillets, skin left on

2 tbsp vegetable oil

TO SERVE

freshly boiled rice

stir-fried vegetables

1 Mix the grated root ginger with the crushed coriander seeds and the chilli powder in a small bowl. Add the lime juice and sesame oil.

2 Place the salmon fillets, skin side down and side by side, on a wide, non-metallic plate or dish. Spoon over the spice mixture, spreading to coat evenly.

3 Cover the dish with clingfilm and chill the salmon in the refrigerator for 30 minutes to let the flavours penetrate.

4 Pour the oil into a wide, heavy-based frying pan or ridged grill pan and heat it to a high temperature. Place the salmon on the hot pan, skin side down.

5 Cook the salmon for 4–5 minutes, without turning, until the fillets are crusty underneath and the flesh flakes easily. Transfer immediately to warmed plates and serve at once with the boiled rice and stir-fried vegetables.

COOK'S TIP

It is important to use a frying pan or a ridged grill pan for this recipe, so the fish cooks evenly throughout without sticking. If the fish is very thick, turn it carefully to cook on the other side for 2–3 minutes.

Prawn Skewers with Chilli

Whole tiger prawns cook very quickly on a barbecue or under a grill, so they are ideal for summertime cooking, indoors or outside.

NUTRITIONAL INFORMATION

Calories	106	Sugars	8g
Protein	11g	Fat	3g
Carbohydrate	8g	Saturates	1g

 5 mins, plus 2 hrs marinating   6 mins

SERVES 4

INGREDIENTS

1 garlic clove, chopped

1 red bird-eye chilli, deseeded and chopped

1 tbsp tamarind paste

1 tbsp sesame oil

1 tbsp dark soy sauce

2 tbsp lime juice

1 tbsp soft light brown sugar

16 raw tiger prawns

1 lime, cut into wedges

TO SERVE

fresh crusty bread

fresh salad leaves

1 Put the chopped garlic and chilli in a small pan with the tamarind paste, sesame oil, soy sauce, lime juice and sugar. Stir over a low heat until the sugar has completely dissolved, then remove from the heat and leave to cool.

2 Wash and pat dry the prawns and place in a single layer in a wide, non-metallic dish. Spoon the marinade over the prawns and turn them over to coat evenly. Cover the dish with clingfilm and leave to marinate in the refrigerator for at least 2 hours or preferably overnight.

3 When you are almost ready to cook the prawns, soak 4 bamboo or wooden skewers in water for about 20 minutes. Drain and dry the skewers, then thread 4 prawns onto each skewer.

4 Grill the skewered prawns under a preheated hot grill for 5–6 minutes, turning them once, until they turn pink and begin to brown. Alternatively, barbecue over hot coals.

5 Thread a wedge of lime onto the end of each skewer and serve with fresh crusty bread and salad leaves.

Chicken Jalfrezi

This is a quick and tasty way of using leftover roast chicken. The sauce can also be used to accompany any cooked poultry, lamb or beef.

NUTRITIONAL INFORMATION

Calories 270	Sugars 3g	
Protein 36g	Fat 11g	
Carbohydrate 7g	Saturates 2g	

  25 mins   15 mins

SERVES 4

I N G R E D I E N T S

1 tsp mustard oil

3 tbsp vegetable oil

1 large onion, finely chopped

3 garlic cloves, crushed

1 tbsp tomato purée

2 tomatoes, skinned and chopped

1 tsp ground turmeric

½ tsp cumin seeds, ground

½ tsp coriander seeds, ground

½ tsp chilli powder

½ tsp garam masala

1 tsp red wine vinegar

1 small red pepper, deseeded and chopped

125 g/4½ oz frozen broad beans

500 g/1 lb 2 oz cooked chicken, cut into bite-sized pieces

salt

sprigs of fresh coriander, to garnish

freshly cooked basmati rice, to serve

1 Heat the mustard oil in a large frying pan set over a high heat for about 1 minute until it begins to smoke.

2 Add the vegetable oil, lower the heat and then add the onion and the garlic. Cook them gently until they are softened and golden.

3 Add the tomato purée, chopped tomatoes, turmeric, ground cumin and coriander seeds, chilli powder, garam masala and red wine vinegar to the frying pan. Stir the mixture over the heat until fragrant.

4 Add the red pepper and broad beans and stir for 2 minutes until the pepper is softened. Stir in the chicken and add salt to taste.

5 Simmer gently for 6–8 minutes until the chicken is heated through and the beans are tender.

6 Serve immediately, garnished with fresh coriander sprigs and accompanied by freshly cooked basmati rice.

Chicken & Mango Stir-fry

This dish has a colourful, exotic mix of flavours that works surprisingly well. It is easy and quick to cook – ideal for a midweek family meal.

NUTRITIONAL INFORMATION

Calories	200	Sugars	........5g
Protein	.......23g	Fat	..........6g
Carbohydrate	....7g	Saturates	.......1g

  15 mins   15 mins

SERVES 4

I N G R E D I E N T S

6 skinless, boneless chicken thighs

2 tsp grated fresh root ginger

1 garlic clove, crushed

1 small red chilli, deseeded

1 large red pepper

4 spring onions

200 g/7 oz mangetouts

100 g/3½ oz baby corn cobs

1 large, firm, ripe mango

2 tbsp sunflower oil

1 tbsp light soy sauce

3 tbsp rice wine or sherry

1 tsp sesame oil

salt and pepper

snipped chives, to garnish

1 Cut the chicken into long, thin strips and place in a bowl. Mix together the ginger, garlic and chilli, then stir into the chicken strips to coat them evenly.

2 Slice the red pepper thinly, then cut it diagonally. Trim the spring onions and slice them diagonally. Cut the mangetouts and corn cobs in half diagonally. Peel the mango, remove the stone and slice thinly.

3 Heat the oil in a large frying pan or wok over a high heat. Add the chicken and stir-fry for 4–5 minutes until just turning golden brown. Add the red pepper and stir-fry over a medium heat for 4–5 minutes to soften.

4 Add the spring onions, mangetouts and baby corn cobs and stir-fry for an additional minute.

5 Mix together the soy sauce, rice wine or sherry, and sesame oil and stir into the wok. Add the mango and stir gently for 1 minute to heat thoroughly.

6 Adjust the seasoning with salt and pepper to taste and serve immediately, garnished with chives.

Chicken with Vinegar

Roasted garlic and mixed spices give an evocative flavour to this tangy chicken dish, a speciality of Valladolid in the Yucatan peninsula.

NUTRITIONAL INFORMATION

Calories 313   Sugars 6g
Protein . . . . .15g   Fat 22g
Carbohydrate . . .14g   Saturates 3g

20 mins, plus 1 hr marinating   25 mins

SERVES 4

I N G R E D I E N T S

8 small, boned chicken thighs

about 600–700 ml/1–1¼ pints chicken stock

15–20 garlic cloves, unpeeled

1 tsp coarsely ground black pepper

½ tsp ground cloves

2 tsp crumbled dried oregano or ½ tsp crushed or powdered bay leaves

½ tsp salt

1 tbsp lime juice

1 tsp cumin seeds, lightly toasted

1 tbsp flour, plus extra for dredging the chicken

3–4 onions, thinly sliced

2 chillies, preferably mildish yellow ones, such as Mexican güero or similar Turkish or Greek chillies, deseeded and sliced

250 ml/9 fl oz vegetable oil

100 ml/3½ fl oz cider vinegar or sherry vinegar

1 Place the chicken in a pan with enough stock to cover. Bring to the boil, then lower the heat and simmer for 5 minutes. Remove from the heat and let the chicken cool and continue to cook in the stock.

2 Meanwhile, roast the garlic cloves in a dry frying pan until they are lightly browned on all sides and tender inside. Leave to cool, then squeeze the flesh from the skins.

3 Grind together the garlic, black pepper, cloves, oregano, salt, lime juice and ¾ teaspoon of the cumin seeds. Add 1 tablespoon of flour.

4 When the chicken is cool, remove from the stock and pat dry. Reserve the stock. Rub the chicken with about two-thirds of the garlic-spice paste and then marinate for between 1–12 hours in the refrigerator.

5 Cook the onions and chillies in a little of the oil until golden brown. Pour in the vinegar and remaining cumin seeds, cook for a few minutes, then add the reserved stock and remaining spice paste. Continue to cook, stirring, for 10 minutes.

6 Dredge the chicken in flour. Cook in the remaining oil until lightly browned. Serve with the onion mixture.

Chicken Tikka

The secret of this very popular dish is that small pieces of chicken are marinated for a minimum of 3 hours in yogurt, garlic and fragrant spices.

NUTRITIONAL INFORMATION

Calories 327   Sugars 2g
Protein . . . . .61g   Fat 8g
Carbohydrate . . . .3g   Saturates 1g

15 mins, plus 3 hrs marinating   10 mins

SERVES 6

I N G R E D I E N T S

1 tsp finely chopped fresh root ginger

1 tsp crushed fresh garlic

½ tsp ground coriander

½ tsp ground cumin

1 tsp chilli powder

3 tbsp yogurt

1 tsp salt

2 tbsp lemon juice

a few drops of red food colouring (optional)

1 tbsp tomato purée

1.5 kg/3 lb 5 oz chicken breast

1 onion, sliced

3 tbsp oil

TO SERVE

fresh salad leaves

1 lemon, cut into wedges

warm naan bread

3 Using a sharp knife, cut the chicken into bite-sized pieces. Add the chicken pieces to the spice mixture and toss to coat well. Leave to marinate for as long as possible – for a minimum of 3 hours or, if possible, overnight.

4 Arrange the onion in the bottom of a heatproof dish. Carefully drizzle half of the oil over the onions.

5 Arrange the marinated chicken pieces on top of the onions and cook under a preheated grill, turning once and basting with the remaining oil, for approximately 10 minutes until the chicken is cooked through and tender.

6 Serve on a bed of fresh salad leaves with warm naan bread, and lemon wedges for squeezing.

1 Mix the ginger, garlic, coriander, cumin and chilli powder thoroughly in a large mixing bowl.

2 Add the yogurt, salt, lemon juice, red food colouring (if using) and tomato purée to the mixing bowl.

 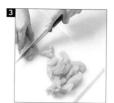 

Crispy Duck with Noodles

This is a robustly flavoured dish that makes a substantial main course.
Serve it with a refreshing cucumber salad or lightly stir-fried vegetables.

NUTRITIONAL INFORMATION

Calories 433	Sugars 7g	
Protein 25g	Fat 10g	
Carbohydrate ...59g	Saturates 2g	

20 mins, plus 1hr marinating

30 mins

SERVES 4

I N G R E D I E N T S

3 duck breasts, total weight about 400 g/14 oz

2 garlic cloves, crushed

1½ tsp chilli paste

1 tbsp honey

3 tbsp dark soy sauce

½ tsp five-spice powder

250 g/9 oz rice stick noodles

1 tsp vegetable oil

1 tsp sesame oil

2 spring onions, sliced

100 g/3½ oz mangetouts

2 tbsp tamarind juice

sesame seeds, to garnish

1 Prick the skin of the duck breasts all over with a fork. Place in a deep dish.

2 Mix together the garlic, chilli paste, honey, soy sauce and five-spice, then pour it over the duck breasts. Turn to coat evenly, then cover and marinate in the refrigerator for at least 1 hour.

3 Meanwhile, soak the rice noodles in hot water for 15 minutes. Drain well.

4 Using a slotted spoon, lift the duck breasts from the marinade (reserve the marinade). Cook on a rack under a hot grill for about 10 minutes, turning occasionally, until they become a rich golden brown. Transfer the duck breasts to a plate, slice thinly, and keep warm until needed.

5 Heat the vegetable and sesame oils in a frying pan, add the sliced spring onions and the mangetouts, and toss for 2 minutes. Stir in the reserved marinade and the tamarind juice and bring to the boil.

6 Add the sliced duck and the noodles to the frying pan and toss to heat them thoroughly. Serve immediately, sprinkled with sesame seeds to garnish.

Hot Beef & Coconut Curry

The heat of the chilli in this curry is balanced and softened by the coconut milk, producing a creamy-textured, rich and lavishly spiced dish.

NUTRITIONAL INFORMATION

Calories 230   Sugars 6g
Protein . . . . .29g   Fat 10g
Carbohydrate . . . .8g   Saturates 3g

15 mins   40 mins

SERVES 4

I N G R E D I E N T S

400 ml/14 fl oz coconut milk

2 tbsp Thai red curry paste

2 garlic cloves, crushed

500 g/1lb 2 oz braising steak

2 kaffir lime leaves, shredded

3 tbsp kaffir lime juice

2 tbsp Thai fish sauce

1 large red chilli, deseeded and sliced

½ tsp turmeric

½ tsp salt

2 tbsp chopped fresh basil

2 tbsp chopped fresh coriander

shredded coconut, to garnish

boiled rice, to serve

1 Bring the coconut milk to the boil in a large pan. Lower the heat, then simmer gently for 10 minutes to thicken. Stir in the red curry paste and garlic and simmer for an additional 5 minutes.

2 Cut the beef into 2-cm/³⁄₄-inch chunks and add them to the pan. Bring the curry to the boil, stirring constantly, then lower the heat.

3 Add the lime leaves, lime juice, fish sauce, chilli, turmeric and salt. Cover the pan and simmer for 20–25 minutes until the meat is tender, adding a little water if the sauce looks too dry.

4 Stir in the fresh basil and coriander and adjust the seasoning to taste. Sprinkle the curry with coconut and serve immediately with boiled rice.

COOK'S TIP

This recipe uses one of the larger, milder red chilli peppers – either fresno or Dutch – simply because they give more colour to the dish. If you prefer to use small Thai, or bird-eye, chillies, you will still need only one because they are much hotter.

Thai-style Burgers

If your family likes to eat burgers, try these – they have a much more interesting flavour than conventional hamburgers.

NUTRITIONAL INFORMATION

Calories	358	Sugars	.........1g
Protein	........23g	Fat	..........29g
Carbohydrate	....2g	Saturates	.......5g

15 mins   8 mins

SERVES 4

I N G R E D I E N T S

1 small lemon grass stalk

1 small red chilli, deseeded

2 garlic cloves, peeled

2 spring onions

200 g/7 oz closed-cup mushrooms

400 g/14 oz minced pork

1 tbsp Thai fish sauce

3 tbsp chopped fresh coriander

sunflower oil, for shallow frying

2 tbsp mayonnaise

1 tbsp lime juice

salt and pepper

TO SERVE

4 sesame hamburger buns

shredded Chinese leaves

1 Place the lemon grass, chilli, garlic and spring onions in a food processor and process to a smooth paste. Add the mushrooms to the food processor and process until they are chopped very finely.

2 Add the minced pork, fish sauce and coriander. Season well with salt and pepper, then divide the mixture into 4 equal portions and use lightly floured hands to shape them into flat burger shapes.

3 Heat the oil in a frying pan over a medium heat. Add the burgers to the pan and cook for 6–8 minutes until they are done to your taste.

4 Meanwhile, mix the mayonnaise with the lime juice. Split the hamburger buns and spread the lime-flavoured mayonnaise on the cut surfaces. Add a few shredded Chinese leaves, top with a burger and sandwich together. Serve immediately while still hot.

COOK'S TIP

Add a spoonful of your favourite relish to each burger or add a few pieces of crisp pickled vegetables for a change of texture.

Fragrant Black Bean Chilli

Enjoy this chilli bean stew Mexican style with soft tortillas, or Californian-style in a bowl with crisp tortilla chips crumbled in.

NUTRITIONAL INFORMATION

Calories 428   Sugars 11g
Protein . . . . .31g   Fat 10g
Carbohydrate . . .53g   Saturates 2g

 20 mins   2½ hrs

SERVES 4

I N G R E D I E N T S

400 g/14 oz dried black beans, soaked overnight and drained

2 tbsp olive oil

1 onion, chopped

5 garlic cloves, roughly chopped

2 rashers bacon, diced (optional)

½–1 tsp ground cumin

½–1 tsp mild red chilli powder

1 red pepper, deseeded and diced

1 carrot, diced

400 g/14 oz tomatoes, canned and chopped, or fresh and diced

1 bunch fresh coriander, roughly chopped

salt and pepper

1 Put the beans in a pan, cover with water and bring to the boil. Boil for 10 minutes, lower the heat and simmer for 1½ hours until tender. Drain well, reserving 225 ml/8 fl oz of the cooking liquid.

2 Heat the oil in a frying pan. Add the onion and garlic and cook for about 2 minutes, stirring. Stir in the bacon, if using, and cook, stirring occasionally, until the bacon is cooked and the onion is soft.

3 Stir in the cumin and chilli powder and cook for a few seconds. Add the red pepper, carrot and tomatoes. Cook over a medium heat for 5 minutes.

4 Add half the coriander and the beans with their reserved liquid. Season with salt and pepper. Simmer for about 30–45 minutes or until thickened.

5 Stir through the remaining coriander, adjust the seasoning to taste and serve at once.

COOK'S TIP

For speed you could use canned beans: drain off the liquid from the can and use 225 ml/8 fl oz water for the liquid added in step 4.

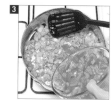

Spicy Pork with Prunes

Prunes add an earthy, wine flavour to this spicy stew. Serve with corn tortillas or crusty bread to dip into the rich sauce.

NUTRITIONAL INFORMATION

Calories 352   Sugars 1g
Protein . . . . .39g   Fat 12g
Carbohydrate . . .24g   Saturates 9g

 🌾 🌾 🌾

15 mins,
plus 8 hrs   ⏲ 3 hrs 50 mins
marinating

SERVES 4–6

INGREDIENTS

1.5 kg/3 lb 5 oz pork joint, such as leg
   or shoulder

juice of 2–3 limes

10 garlic cloves, chopped

3–4 tbsp mild chilli powder, such as ancho
   or New Mexico

4 tbsp vegetable oil

2 onions, chopped

500 ml/18 fl oz chicken stock

25 small, tart tomatoes, roughly chopped

25 prunes, stoned

1–2 tsp sugar

pinch of ground cinnamon

pinch of ground mixed spice

pinch of ground cumin

salt

warmed corn tortillas, to serve

1 Combine the pork with the lime juice, garlic, chilli powder and half the oil in a non-metallic bowl. Season with salt. Cover and refrigerate overnight.

2 Remove the pork from the marinade, wipe dry with kitchen paper and reserve the marinade. Heat the remaining oil in a flameproof casserole and brown the pork evenly until just golden. Add the onions, marinade and the stock. Cover and cook in a preheated oven, 180°C/350°F/Gas Mark 4, for 2–3 hours until tender.

3 Spoon off the fat from the surface of the cooking liquid and add the tomatoes. Continue to cook for 20 minutes or until the tomatoes are tender. Mash the tomatoes into a coarse paste. Add the prunes, sugar and spices to taste.

4 Increase the oven temperature to 200°C/400°F/Gas Mark 6. Cook the meat and sauce in the oven, uncovered, for 20–30 minutes until the meat has browned and the juices have thickened.

5 Remove the meat from the pan and leave to stand for a few minutes. Carve into thin slices and spoon the sauce over the top. Serve with warm tortillas.

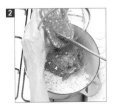

Wild Mushroom Vermicelli

Simple to make, this spicy dish has Spanish chorizo sausage and anchovies as its main ingredients, and will set the taste buds tingling.

NUTRITIONAL INFORMATION

Calories	495	Sugars	. . . . .1g
Protein	. . . . .15g	Fat	. . . . .35g
Carbohydrate	. . .33g	Saturates	. . . . . . .5g

 5 mins   10 mins

SERVES 6

I N G R E D I E N T S

680 g/1½ lb dried vermicelli

125 ml/4 fl oz olive oil

2 garlic cloves, finely chopped

125 g/4½ oz chorizo, sliced

225 g/8 oz wild mushrooms

3 fresh red chillies, deseeded and chopped

2 tbsp freshly grated Parmesan cheese

salt and pepper

10 anchovy fillets, to garnish

1 Bring a large pan of lightly salted water to the boil. Add the vermicelli and 1 tablespoon of the oil and cook until just tender but still firm to the bite. Drain, place on a large, warm serving plate and keep warm.

2 Meanwhile heat the remaining oil in a large frying pan. Add the garlic and cook for 1 minute. Add the chorizo and wild mushrooms and cook for 4 minutes, then add the chopped red chillies and cook for another minute until the mushrooms are just cooked through.

3 Pour the chorizo and wild mushroom mixture over the vermicelli and season with a little salt and pepper. Sprinkle over the freshly grated Parmesan cheese, garnish with the anchovy fillets and then serve immediately.

COOK'S TIP
Always obtain wild mushrooms from a reliable source and never pick them yourself unless you are absolutely certain of their identity.

Lamb Couscous

Couscous is a North African speciality. It is usually accompanied by a spicy mixture of meat and fruit, which adds a note of luxury.

NUTRITIONAL INFORMATION

Calories . . . . . . .647 Sugars 22g
Protein . . . . .41g Fat 21g
Carbohydrate . . .79g Saturates 6g

 20 mins   20 mins

SERVES 4

I N G R E D I E N T S

2 tbsp olive oil

500 g/1 lb 2 oz lean lamb fillet, thinly sliced

2 onions, sliced

2 garlic cloves, chopped

1 cinnamon stick

1 tsp ground ginger

1 tsp paprika

½ tsp chilli powder

600 ml/1 pint hot chicken stock

3 carrots, thinly sliced

2 turnips, halved and sliced

400 g/14 oz canned chopped tomatoes

2 tbsp raisins

425 g/15 oz canned chickpeas, drained and rinsed

3 courgettes, sliced

125 g/4½ oz fresh dates, halved and stoned, or 125 g/4½ oz dried apricots

300 g/10½ oz couscous

600 ml/1 pint boiling water

salt

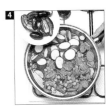

1 Heat the oil in a frying pan and cook the lamb briskly for 3 minutes until browned. Remove from the frying pan with a slotted spoon and set aside.

2 Add the onions to the pan and cook, stirring constantly, until soft. Add the garlic and spices and cook for 1 minute.

3 Add the stock, carrots, turnips, tomatoes, raisins, chickpeas and lamb, and salt to taste. Cover, bring to the boil and simmer for 12 minutes.

4 Add the courgettes and the dates. Cover again and cook for 8 minutes.

5 Meanwhile, put the couscous in a bowl with 1 teaspoon of salt and pour the boiling water over it. Leave to soak for 5 minutes then fluff it with a fork.

6 To serve, pile the couscous onto a warmed serving platter and make a hollow in the centre. Put the meat and vegetables in the hollow (discard the cinnamon stick), and pour some sauce over it. Serve the rest of the sauce separately.

Spiced Lamb & Lentils

This recipe makes a hearty, warming winter curry. Gram lentils are used in this recipe but split yellow peas make a tasty alternative.

NUTRITIONAL INFORMATION

Calories 397   Sugars 1g
Protein . . . . .42g   Fat 22g
Carbohydrate . . . .8g   Saturates 9g

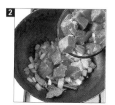

20 mins, plus
6 hrs soaking   1¼ hrs

SERVES 4

I N G R E D I E N T S

2 tbsp oil

1 tsp cumin seeds

2 bay leaves

2.5-cm/1-inch piece cinnamon stick

1 onion, chopped

750 g/1 lb 10 oz lean, boneless lamb, cut into 2.5-cm/1-inch cubes

125 g/4½ oz split gram lentils, soaked for 6 hours and drained

1 tsp salt

1 fresh green chilli, deseeded and sliced

1.3 litres/2¼ pints water

1 garlic clove, crushed

¼ tsp ground turmeric

1 tsp chilli powder

½ tsp garam masala or curry powder (optional)

1 tbsp chopped fresh coriander (optional)

naan bread and pickles, to serve

1 Heat the oil in a balti pan or a wok, add the cumin seeds, bay leaves and cinnamon stick, and cook over a high heat until the cumin seeds start popping.

2 Add the onion and stir-fry until golden brown. Add the cubed lamb to the pan and stir-fry until evenly browned.

3 Add the lentils, salt, chilli, water, garlic, turmeric and chilli powder and stir well. Bring the mixture to the boil then simmer for 1 hour, stirring occasionally.

4 Season with garam masala, if using, and cook for another 5 minutes. Remove and discard the cinnamon stick.

5 Stir in the chopped coriander, if using, and serve with naan bread and pickles.

COOK'S TIP

To save time on soaking, use 400 g/14 oz canned lentils. These should be added to the curry when it has finished cooking. Heat through gently until the lentils are hot, then garnish and serve.

Melon & Ginger Crush

A really refreshing summer drink, this melon crush is quick and simple to make. Use ordinary limes if you cannot find kaffir limes.

NUTRITIONAL INFORMATION

Calories 46   Sugars 7g
Protein ....1g   Fat 0g
Carbohydrate ....7g   Saturates 0g

🍧 5 mins   ⏱ 0 mins

SERVES 4

I N G R E D I E N T S

1 melon, about 800 g/1 lb 12 oz

6 tbsp ginger wine

3 tbsp kaffir lime juice

crushed ice

1 lime

1 Peel and deseed the melon and roughly chop the flesh. Place it in a blender or food processor with the ginger wine and the lime juice.

2 Blend on high speed until the mixture is completely smooth.

3 Put plenty of crushed ice into 4 tall glasses. Pour the melon and ginger crush over the ice.

4 Cut the lime into slim slices, cut a slit in each one and slip one onto the rim of each glass. Serve immediately.

VARIATION

For a non-alcoholic version of this drink, omit the ginger wine then top up the glass with ginger ale. For a seasonal change of flavour, use a watermelon.

Lychee & Ginger Sorbet

A refreshing dessert after a rich meal, this quick and simple sorbet can be served alone or with fruit salad.

NUTRITIONAL INFORMATION

Calories 159   Sugars 40g
Protein . . . . .2g   Fat 0g
Carbohydrate . . .40g   Saturates 0g

5 mins,
plus 5–6 hrs
freezing

0 mins

SERVES 4

I N G R E D I E N T S

800 g/1 lb 12 oz canned lychees in syrup

zest of 1 lime, finely grated

2 tbsp lime juice

3 tbsp crystallised ginger syrup

2 egg whites

TO DECORATE

starfruit slices

slivers of crystallised ginger

1 Drain the lychees, reserving the syrup. Place the fruits in a blender or a food processor with the lime zest, lime juice and crystallised ginger syrup and process until completely smooth. Transfer to a mixing bowl and pour in the reserved lychee syrup.

2 To make the sorbet, pour the mixture into a freezerproof container and freeze for 1–1½ hours until slushy in texture. Remove from the freezer and whisk to break up the ice crystals. Whisk the egg whites in a clean, dry bowl until they rise in stiff peaks, then fold quickly and lightly into the iced mixture. Return the mixture to the freezer and freeze until firm. Alternatively, to save time, replace the whole procedure in this step by processing the mixture quickly in an ice-cream maker.

3 When ready to serve, remove the sorbet from the freezer and place in the refrigerator 20 minutes before needed. Serve in scoops, decorated with slices of starfruit and slivers of crystallised ginger.

COOK'S TIP

It is not recommended that raw egg whites are served to very young children, pregnant women, the elderly or anyone weakened by chronic illness.